THIS  ANNUAL
BELONGS TO

AGE

FAVOURITE TEAM

FAVOURITE PLAYER

TEAM I PLAY FOR

POSITION I PLAY

PROFILE PICTURE

SHOOT!

THE VOICE OF FOOTBALL

ANNUAL EDITOR: Dan Tyler & Sam Horscraft

CONTRIBUTORS: Sam Carroll, Daniel Defalco, Callum Ferguson, Charlie Parker-Turner, Charlie Scott

f /TheVoiceOfFootball   WWW.SHOOT.CO.UK   🐦 @_shootfootball

CONTENTS

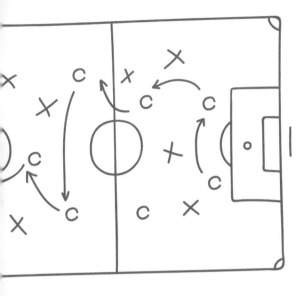

BUILD YOUR CLUB

Football needs you! A club has dropped out of the league. Can you create a new one to replace it?

TEAM NAME _the best Team in world_

STADIUM NAME _best traffrd_

NICKNAME _thebest_

CLUB BADGE

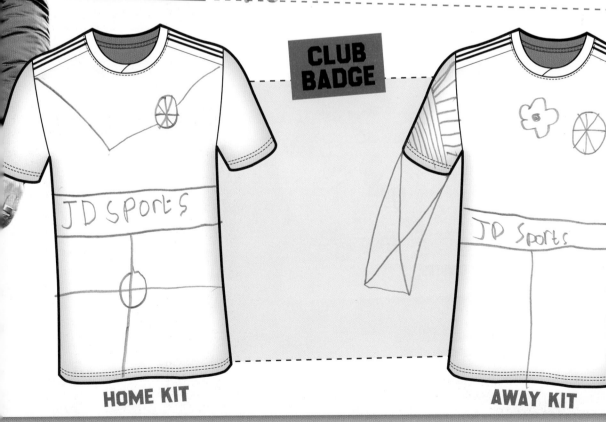

HOME KIT

AWAY KIT

KNOW YOUR NATIONS

SON HEUNG-MIN

COUNTRY:

Every footballer dreams of playing for their country. Here we have seven regular internationals. Match up each player to the country they play for.

ANSWERS ON PAGE 76

PAULO DYBALA

COUNTRY:

CHRISTIAN PULISIC

COUNTRY:

PIERRE-EMERICK AUBAMEYANG

COUNTRY:

MAT RYAN

COUNTRY:

ISCO

COUNTRY:

MARQUINHOS

COUNTRY:

 SPAIN

 SOUTH KOREA

 USA

 ARGENTINA

 GABON

 AUSTRALIA

 BRAZIL

WORLD CUP WORDSEARCH

The World Cup is the biggest football tournament on the planet. Every four years the best international teams go head-to-head for the game's top prize.

Can you find all the teams to have won the men's and women's World Cups below.

ANSWERS ON PAGE 76

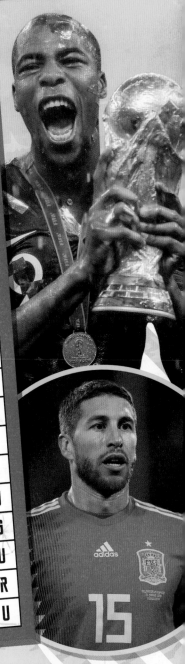

D	D	C	J	I	S	L	S	J	R	A	E	Y	Q	O	W	F	B	T	E
Y	B	K	R	G	I	T	W	Z	B	Y	R	Q	K	Q	U	P	L	H	B
K	G	J	J	Z	E	Z	L	H	M	K	C	G	O	U	U	D	E	B	T
K	F	O	A	R	O	A	D	O	K	G	M	P	E	N	K	C	R	I	L
N	V	R	L	P	T	O	L	W	W	W	T	O	D	N	I	D	Y	E	Z
O	B	I	E	X	K	Y	J	F	B	I	M	P	G	E	T	M	Z	J	L
J	N	E	E	K	L	E	I	T	A	L	Y	W	S	K	I	I	R	O	N
G	O	U	D	Y	W	I	T	O	V	G	U	L	Q	S	U	J	N	I	F
D	L	S	X	G	K	S	V	M	Q	V	U	A	E	F	W	J	K	A	F
A	I	A	N	Q	F	F	P	T	P	W	N	O	R	W	A	Y	R	Y	C
S	M	O	Q	G	X	Q	T	A	D	N	G	W	S	J	W	Y	L	O	K
K	D	F	R	A	N	C	E	E	I	A	E	D	A	S	Z	Y	R	S	C
I	T	D	D	F	K	J	C	I	O	N	R	W	S	Y	I	T	N	S	I
K	A	T	Y	O	X	M	B	K	S	D	M	Y	O	L	N	E	J	M	Y
I	S	S	E	M	A	Z	J	A	R	J	A	W	D	R	T	E	D	U	A
M	N	T	Z	T	N	R	U	Z	S	A	N	Q	M	R	D	B	I	U	U
C	S	Q	D	N	Y	K	L	A	D	P	Y	U	E	Y	A	E	C	X	G
L	F	X	J	A	Q	G	O	K	U	A	T	M	U	W	U	E	P	M	U
W	N	E	N	G	L	A	N	D	Y	N	E	D	L	E	C	I	Z	N	R
D	P	U	O	N	J	K	V	X	N	S	Y	B	B	S	N	C	Z	Y	U

ENGLAND ☐	BRAZIL ☐	ITALY ☐	ARGENTINA ☐	GERMANY ☐
(Men's 1966)	(Men's 1958, 1962, 1970, 1994, 2002)	(Men's 1934, 1938, 1982, 2006)	(Men's 1978, 1986)	(Men's 1954, 1974, 1990, 2014 / Women's 2003, 2007)

FRANCE ☐	SPAIN ☐	URUGUAY ☐	USA ☐	NORWAY ☐	JAPAN ☐
(Men's 1998, 2018)	(Men's 2010)	(Men's 1930, 1950)	(Women's 1991, 1999, 2015)	(Women's 1995)	(Women's 2011)

FACT FILE

POSITION: Right-back
HEIGHT: 1.75m (5ft 9in)
BIRTH DATE: October 7, 1998
PLACE OF BIRTH: Liverpool
CLUB: Liverpool
INTERNATIONAL: England

DID YOU KNOW?

Before making his England debut, Trent was eligible to play for the United States through his grandmother.

TRENT ALEXANDER-ARNOLD

LIVERPOOL'S LOCAL HERO

YOU'LL NEVER WALK ALONE
LIVERPOOL FOOTBALL CLUB
EST·1892

Born just 2.5 miles away from Anfield in West Derby, Liverpool's Trent Alexander-Arnold has firmly established himself as a local hero.

The right-back had a standout 2018/19 season as he helped his boyhood club win their sixth European Cup and finish second to Manchester City in the Premier League.

Trent, who registered a top-flight record 12 assists for a defender, also became a regular in the England national team after being part of the squad which reached the World Cup semi-finals in 2018.

Following another eye-catching year, Shoot spoke exclusively to the talented Scouser on being the Kop's local hero, pulling on the Three Lions shirt, that night in Madrid and playing for Jurgen Klopp.

What's it like to play for the club you support?

"It's a dream come true. Whenever I got the opportunity to go to Anfield I always dreamt of walking out of the tunnel and onto the pitch. When I was young being one of those players seemed so far away. Growing up it was only really Gerrard and Jamie Carragher that came through so I didn't think it would come true. It's very rare for a Scouse kid now to make it at Liverpool but I've always wanted to play for this club and it's the only club I could ever see myself playing for."

What are your earliest memories of watching Liverpool?

"I first watched them at Anfield when we beat Juventus 2-1 in the Champions League in 2005. Since then I knew I would always support Liverpool and that I wanted to play for them. When I couldn't go to Anfield I would watch all of the games on TV. I loved watching them and my favourite players were Steven Gerrard, Jamie Carragher, Javier Mascherano, Xabi Alonso and Fernando Torres."

You take great set pieces for Liverpool and England. Did you practise those growing up?

"I didn't really take them until I was 16. I remember a coach saying that if a player can take set pieces then they have more chance of getting into teams. If two players have the same qualities but one can potentially score or create from set pieces then that player will have more chance of getting picked. I saw that as an opportunity and started to practise them."

How special is it to walk out and play at Anfield?

"Anfield is always special but on a Champions League night there's something a little bit different. As a player you feel that and we almost go into games thinking that we can't be beat. We've shown that against AS Roma and Barcelona in recent seasons. It's a very special place and I try to soak up every minute I play there."

What was it like to win the Champions League 12 months after losing the 2018 final?

"It was a dream come true to win the Champions League with my boyhood club. It was extra special because of the disappointment of losing to Real Madrid the year before. We felt like we owed it to the fans for supporting us through everything. I now just want to win more trophies with this club."

What's it like to pull on an England shirt and to do it at a World Cup?

"As a kid there's nothing better than getting your summer England kit with your favourite player on the back and having that dream of winning a major tournament. So to play for England at Wembley and at a World Cup is something I'd always dreamt of but didn't think would happen. If playing for Liverpool is hard then playing for England is even harder because there's so many top players fighting for a place in the squad. When I get a chance I just give it my all and try to saviour every minute. I just feel really fortunate to have been given the opportunity to play for both England and Liverpool."

What's it like to play for the main man Jurgen Klopp?

"He's a special man and a special manager. The best thing about him is his passion for football. He's really ambitious but he doesn't obsess over results. He wants us to go and express ourselves, have fun and not hold back. He wants us to give back to the fans around the world who give us their dreams and pay so much to see us."

Virgil van Dijk has helped transform Liverpool's defence. How good is he?

"It's hard to describe how good he actually is and how much of a presence he is on the pitch. When people come up against him they're scared of him because he's so big, strong and almost impossible to get past. I don't think I've ever seen anyone get past him in training. Everyone has had a go and it's virtually impossible. He's just someone that dominates on the pitch and will make that interception which sets us on the attack. It's rare that you see so much love for a centre-back but he can win games for us at both ends. The fans love him and we are really happy to have him with us."

How proud were you to be named in the 2019 PFA Team of the Year?

"It's made myself and my family proud. To be voted for by the people you play against every week means it's one of the best honours you can get as a player. I'm proud that players think that I'm the best right-back they have come up against all season. This is something to be cherished as I don't know if it will come around again. Hopefully I can get in there a few more times throughout my career."

You used to play in midfield as a youngster. Do you think you will move back to that position in the future?

"If I'm asked to play in midfield then I'll give it my best shot but the most important thing at the moment is that I'm a right-back. It allows me to influence the game as the modern full-back is one of the most important players on the pitch. I can decide a game at either end, especially the way we play at Liverpool where we always play on the front foot. I'm more than happy to be playing in that position and I just want to stay focussed on improving as a right-back."

Is there an area of your game you are aiming to improve?

"Everything can always be improved but I'd say the defensive side of my game more than anything. I want to become more solid defensively like Virgil is, so people are actually afraid to come up against me. Every defender wants that feeling of being untouchable and if I can work towards that it will only help the team keep clean sheets."

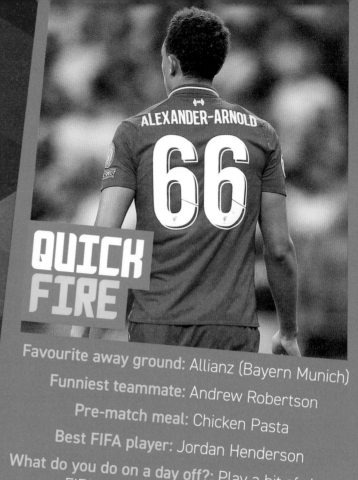

ALEXANDER-ARNOLD 66

QUICK FIRE

Favourite away ground: Allianz (Bayern Munich)
Funniest teammate: Andrew Robertson
Pre-match meal: Chicken Pasta
Best FIFA player: Jordan Henderson
What do you do on a day off?: Play a bit of chess, FIFA, walk my dogs and chill out.

What advice do you give any young Shoot reader dreaming of becoming a professional footballer?

"Enjoy it as much as possible. Don't be afraid to dream about things because dreams do come true. Don't waste a day because each day is an opportunity to get better. Play as much as you can and hopefully one day you'll be lucky enough to be given the chance like I have."

Instagram: @trentarnold66
Twitter: @trentaa98

KIT SWAP

ANSWERS ON PAGE 76

These four players have all been on the same flight. The bad news is that the airport's baggage handlers have mixed up their luggage. Can you sort out the problem and match the correct shirts, shorts and socks to their owner...

A

B

C

D

A

B

C

D

A

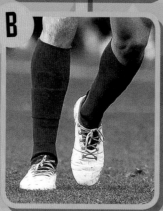

B

C

D

SCOTT BROWN	JAMIE VARDY	SERGE GNABRY	JORDI ALBA
SHIRT ○	SHIRT ○	SHIRT ○	SHIRT ○
SHORTS ○	SHORTS ○	SHORTS ○	SHORTS ○
SOCKS ○	SOCKS ○	SOCKS ○	SOCKS ○

PROLIFIC PARRIS

Nikita Parris is one of the best forwards in world football.

The attacker started her career with Everton before making the move to Manchester City in 2015.

The talented striker went goal crazy in the blue of City, scoring 62 times in 127 matches to help the club win multiple trophies.

Keets' super skills and determination has also seen her become a key player for the England national team, wearing the iconic number 7 shirt.

Now after moving away from the Women's Super League to join Champions League winners Lyon, Shoot highlights some of the Lionesses star's impressive career achievements so far.

2015
Loan move from Everton to Manchester City

PFA Team of the Year

2016
Permanent transfer from Everton to Man City

WSL winner

FA WSL Cup winner

England debut (vs Serbia)

First England goal (vs Serbia)

2017
FA Cup winner

Major international tournament debut (Euro 2017)

First international tournament goal (vs Portugal)

2018
England's top scorer in World Cup qualifying (6 goals)

100th Man City appearance (vs Atletico Madrid)

2019
FA WSL Cup winner

FA Cup winner

FWA Women's Footballer of the Year

PFA Team of the Year

WSL's all-time leading scorer (49 goals)

SheBelieves Cup winner

World Cup debut (vs Scotland)

First World Cup goal (vs Scotland)

FACT FILE
POSITION: Forward

DATE OF BIRTH: March 10, 1994

PLACE OF BIRTH: Toxteth, Liverpool

HEIGHT: 1.62m (5ft 4in)

CLUB: Lyon

INTERNATIONAL: England

DID YOU KNOW?
Parris has a degree in Sports Development from Liverpool John Moores University.

Instagram: @nikitaparris17
Twitter: @lilkeets

SOUTHGATE'S SECRET SELECTION

Gareth Southgate has tried to keep his team selection secret before the big match. Can you use the code to reveal the England manager's starting XI.

ANSWERS ON PAGE 76

A

B

C

D

E

F

G

H

I

J

K

L

M

N

O

P

Q

R

S

T

U

V

W

X

Y

Z

GARETH'S XI:

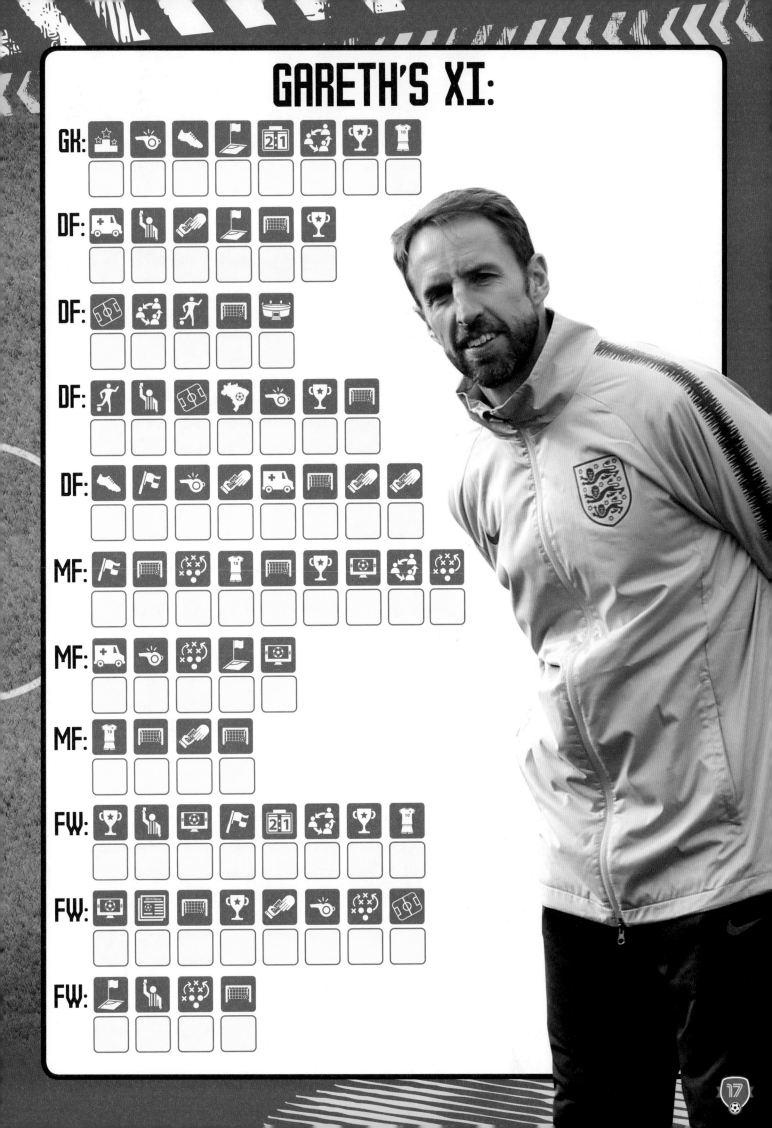

GK: ☐ ☐ ☐ ☐ ☐ ☐ ☐ ☐

DF: ☐ ☐ ☐ ☐ ☐ ☐

DF: ☐ ☐ ☐ ☐ ☐

DF: ☐ ☐ ☐ ☐ ☐ ☐ ☐

DF: ☐ ☐ ☐ ☐ ☐ ☐ ☐ ☐

MF: ☐ ☐ ☐ ☐ ☐ ☐ ☐ ☐ ☐

MF: ☐ ☐ ☐ ☐ ☐

MF: ☐ ☐ ☐ ☐

FW: ☐ ☐ ☐ ☐ ☐ ☐ ☐ ☐

FW: ☐ ☐ ☐ ☐ ☐ ☐ ☐ ☐

FW: ☐ ☐ ☐ ☐

Manchester City and their fans will never forget the 2018/19 season. Pep Guardiola's side became the first men's team to win the domestic treble of Premier League, FA Cup and League Cup. In a squad full of superstars from all corners of the globe, it was Englishman Raheem Sterling who was one of the Cityzens' top performers.

RAHEEM STERLING

A STERLING YEAR

MANCHESTER 18 94 CITY

After helping the Three Lions reach the World Cup semi-finals, the forward returned to the Etihad where he scored goal after goal and collected some very special personal awards. To celebrate the prolific wide man's sensational campaign, Shoot takes a look back at Sterling's stellar moments....

FACT FILE

POSITION: Forward
HEIGHT: 1.70m (5ft 7in)
BIRTH DATE: December 8, 1994
BIRTH PLACE: Kingston, Jamaica
CLUB: Manchester City
INTERNATIONAL: England

HIGHLIGHTS

AUGUST 2018
50th Premier League goal in 2-0 win at Arsenal

OCTOBER 2018
Two goals in 3-2 win vs Spain

NOVEMBER 2018
50th City goal (City 6-1 Southampton)

FEBRUARY 2019
Signs new three-year contract

Two goals in 6-0 win vs Chelsea

Scores winning penalty in League Cup final vs Chelsea

STATS

GAMES
56

GOALS
31
(most in a season)

Premier League: 17

FA Cup: 3
(most in a season)

Champions League: 5
(most in a season)

England: 6
(most in a season)

ASSISTS
17
(most in a season)

MARCH 2019
Scores quickest Premier League hat-trick of the season (13 minutes) vs Watford

MARCH 2019
First England hat-trick (vs Czech Republic)

APRIL 2019
PFA Young Player of the Year & PFA Team of the Year

DID YOU KNOW?
Sterling arranged for 500 pupils from his old school (Ark Elvin Academy) to attend the FA Cup semi-final between City and Brighton at Wembley Stadium.

MAY 2019
FWA Footballer of the Year
Two goals in 6–0 FA Cup final win vs Watford

Instagram: @sterling7
Twitter: @sterling7

DREAM TEAM

There are lots of top-class players but which do you think would make the best team in the world? Write down your Dream XI on the teamsheet below.

TIP
A 4-3-3 formation requires quick full backs to run up and down the wings.

YOUR SQUAD:

1 ....

2 ....

3 ....

4 ....

5 ....

6 ....

7 ....

8 ....

9 ....

10 ....

11 ....

LEGENDS

QUICK FIRE

David Seaman is simply one of the finest goalkeepers England has ever had. The super stopper won 75 caps for the Three Lions and played at four major tournaments. At club level he is best known for his time with Arsenal. Seaman represented the Gunners 564 times and helped the North London club win nine major trophies.

Now, nearly 16 years after hanging up his gloves, Shoot put the Yorkshireman's reflexes to the test once again with 10 quick-fire questions....

BEST PLAYER YOU'VE PLAYED WITH?
Thierry Henry for Arsenal and Paul Gascoigne for England

FAVOURITE MATCH YOU PLAYED IN?
England vs Spain in the Euro '96 quarter-final at Wembley.

BEST CAREER SAVE?
From Paul Peschisolido's header in the 2003 FA Cup semi-final. I was 39 at the time.

VAR OR NO VAR?
VAR

CAREER HIGHS?
Euro '96 with England and the two double winning seasons with Arsenal.

MESSI OR RONALDO?
Ronaldo.

2019/20 PREMIER LEAGUE WINNER?
Sorry Arsenal fans but I have to say Liverpool.

2019/20 PLAYER TO WATCH?
I think Mo Salah is going to be the star of the Premier League.

FAVOURITE STADIUM YOU PLAYED AT?
Old Wembley Stadium. Great memories and great history.

FAVOURITE MANAGER YOU PLAYED FOR?
Arsene Wenger for Arsenal and Terry Venables for England.

Seaman spoke to *Shoot* ahead of taking part in Soccer Aid for Uncief 2019.
For more information or to donate head to socceraid.org.uk

WHO AM I?

Use the clues to see if you can name the three mystery football stars...

ANSWERS ON PAGE 76

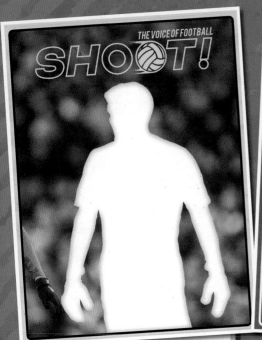

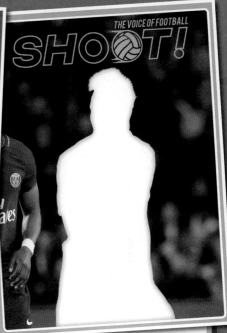

PLAYER 1

CLUE 1:
I'm a goalkeeper.

CLUE 2:
I'm a trained chef.

CLUE 3:
I've played with Cristiano Ronaldo, Salomon Rondon and Troy Deeney at club level.

CLUE 4:
I've played in non-league and the Champions League.

CLUE 5:
I've got more than one England cap.

....

....

PLAYER 2

CLUE 1:
I'm a midfielder.

CLUE 2:
I have captained my country.

CLUE 3:
I've played with Alexis Sanchez, Emre Can and Cesc Fabregas at club level.

CLUE 4:
I've scored two FA Cup final winning goals.

CLUE 5:
I've recently moved from London to Turin.

....

....

PLAYER 3

CLUE 1:
I'm a striker.

CLUE 2:
I took a selfie when celebrating a goal.

CLUE 3:
I've played with David Silva, Zlatan Imbrahimovic and Steven Gerrard at club level.

CLUE 4:
I set-up a Premier League title winning goal in 2012.

CLUE 5:
I've got multiple Italy caps.

....

....

23

DID YOU KNOW?

The beautiful game is full of magical stories. You may think you're a bit of a football 'know-it-all' but here's 10 more amazing facts to impress your mates with.

UNDER CONSTRUCTION

The 2022 World Cup final will be played in Lusail, Qatar. We would include a picture but the city has not been built yet. To be continued.

Birmingham City were the first English club to play in Europe in 1955. So you can forget about Liverpool, Chelsea and Manchester United…

Brazil's first ever official match was against Exeter City in 1914. The South Americans won 2-0. We guess the visitors would take that scoreline now.

YOU COULDN'T PLAY YOUR OWN TEAM IN A CUP FINAL, COULD YOU? WELL REAL MADRID DID IN 1980 WHEN THEIR B TEAM REACHED THE SPANISH CUP FINAL. UNSURPRISINGLY THE A TEAM WON 6-1.

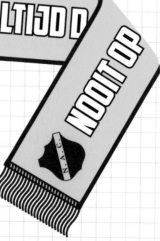

The longest football club name in the world is **NOOIT OPGEVEN ALTIJD DOORZETTEN, AANGENAAM DOOR VERMAAK EN NUTTIG DOOR ONTSPANNING, COMBINATIE BREDA.** This stands for Dutch club NAC Breda. We bet commentators are happy it has been shortened.

Neymar Jr's £198m move from Barcelona to Paris Saint-Germain made him the world's most expensive player. The first ever recorded transfer was Willie Groves moving from West Bromwich Albion to Aston Villa for £100 in 1893. How times have changed.

The fastest player in the 2018/19 Premier League was Timothy Fosu-Mensah. The defender was recorded sprinting 21.95mph for Fulham. It's a shame the Cottagers couldn't run away from relegation.

21.95 MPH

We all love a great comeback and maybe Charlton Athletic produced the best ever. The Addicks were 6-1 down to Huddersfield in 1957 but six goals in the last 30 minutes saw them win 7-6. Incredible!

Ever thought your team would never end a losing run? Well spare a thought for Andorra. The European nation went 13 years and 86 matches without a win. But a miracle happened when they defeated San Marino 2-0 back in 2017. The fans' patience paid off.

...that have won the Champions League. But the Swedish striker has never won the trophy. We bet he'll have something to say about that!!

WHO WEARS WHAT?

David Beckham in adidas Predators and the Brazilian Ronaldo in Nike's R9 Mercurials... Is it just us that when thinking about iconic players we always remember their boots too?

I guess not. So we've teamed up with the football deals site **FOOTY.COM** to showcase which boots today's top footballing talent wear.

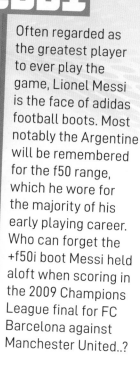

MESSI

Often regarded as the greatest player to ever play the game, Lionel Messi is the face of adidas football boots. Most notably the Argentine will be remembered for the f50 range, which he wore for the majority of his early playing career. Who can forget the +f50i boot Messi held aloft when scoring in the 2009 Champions League final for FC Barcelona against Manchester United..?

GET THE MESSI LOOK

Messi has spent the last few seasons wearing the Nemeziz range, which has been designed for complete mobility in all directions at pace. If you are a pacey attacker, these are the boots for you!

AGUERO

Many football fans will only ever have known Manchester City goalscoring legend Sergio Aguero wearing Puma boots. The Argentine signed a sponsorship deal with the brand back in 2011, shortly after joining the Premier League club from Atletico Madrid.

GET THE AGUERO LOOK

The Puma Ones are the brand's top of the range football boot. Worn by Aguero in the 2018/19 season, the super striker smashed home 21 Premier League goals in them to help City defend their title. Made for natural finishers!

NEYMAR

Silky-Brazilian Neymar Jr. has always been associated with Nike. Even when he was making a name for himself as a talented teenager at Brazilian outfit Santos, the speedy attacker was wearing Nike's Mercurial Vapor boots.

GET THE NEYMAR LOOK

The South American icon is still wearing the Nike Mercurial Vapor range. Designed to give him an edge when gliding across the ground, these boots help the forward dribble past his opponents. If you're light on your feet and can beat a player, these are definitely for you!

RONALDO

The Portuguese megastar sits at the highest level of the game's elite and, being a style icon, his Nike footwear is always hugely popular. The goalscorer spent the early part of his career in Nike Mercurial Vapors, often changing colourways two or three times throughout the season. The year 2010 saw the first boot to be released from the now infamous CR7 range.

GET THE RONALDO LOOK

Ronaldo has been wearing the Superfly Elite boots from the Nike Mercurial range. These boots complement his speed across the ground as well as his deadly shooting prowess. Ideal for quick players with an eye for goal!

MANE

Liverpool star Sadio Mane has recently been the face of New Balance's new Furon 5.0 boot which launched in 2019. In the past the Senegalese forward has worn Nike boots, but it seems he will now stick with the slick design of the New Balance range.

GET THE MANE LOOK

The lightweight New Balance boot is perfect for the wing wizard to weave past defenders. Acceleration is a key design feature, ideal for Mane's electric pace. If you are a speedy attacker, these are the boots you should check out!

POGBA

The first out-and-out midfielder to make our list is the modern-day face of the Predator, Paul Pogba. A creative force in the middle of the park, the talented Frenchman bossed the iconic adidas range as he played a key part in helping France win the 2018 World Cup in Russia. The famous boots also assisted in his best ever goalscoring season as he netted 13 times for Manchester United during the 2018/19 campaign.

GET THE POGBA LOOK

The latest version of the Pogba's adidas Predators are all about control, appealing to the Frenchman who looks to dictate a game. If you are a player who wants to control a match then the adidas Predators are for you.

1

Which club has won the Premier League title the most times?

....

2

England midfielder Declan Rice also played for which other country?

....

3

Name this England super striker...

....

4

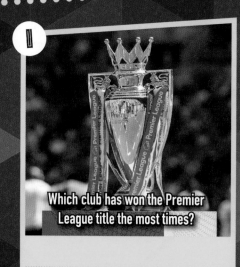

Huddersfield Town, Cardiff City and which other club were relegated from the Premier League in 2019?

....

5

Name the 2019 PFA Player of the Year Award winner...

....

6

Leicester City manager Brendan Rodgers is from which country?

....

7

Which team won the 2019 Women's Super League?

....

8

In which country are the club Eintracht Frankfurt from?

....

9

Name this Champions League winning manager...

....

QUIZ

Do you think you know your football? Then put your knowledge to the test in the first half of our ultimate quiz. You get one point for each correct answer and some can be found in the rest of the annual.

ANSWERS ON PAGE 76

10
Which England women's star has played for Sunderland, Everton, Liverpool, Man City and Lyon?

11
Newcastle United would play which club in the Tyne-Wear derby?

12
Have Ajax won 30, 32 or 34 Dutch League titles?

13
Which country does midfield star Christian Eriksen play for?

14
Which French team has won the Women's Champions League the past four seasons?

15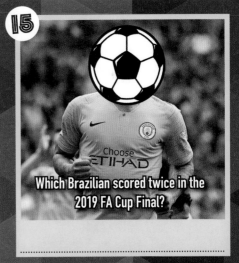
Which Brazilian scored twice in the 2019 FA Cup Final?

16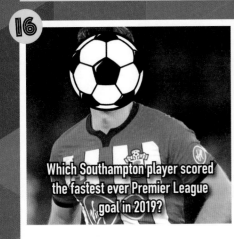
Which Southampton player scored the fastest ever Premier League goal in 2019?

17
Name the stadium where Leeds United play their home games...

18
Mohamed Salah, Sadio Mane and who shared the 2018/19 Premier League Golden Boot?

THE SECOND HALF KICKS OFF ON PAGE 68

29

GUNN'S GUIDE TO GOAL KEEPING

Want to become a Premier League goalkeeper like Angus Gunn? The Southampton and England Under-21 international spoke to *Shoot* about his top 10 goalkeeping tips for keeping the ball out of the net.

What is the best drill to get a goalkeeper prepared for matches?

There's so many goalkeeping drills which can help you improve areas of your game but I think the best thing you can do is to play in a game situation as much as possible. I find playing matches in training is the best way to help me improve because they are the closest I get to playing in a real game.

DID YOU KNOW?

Angus's dad is Norwich City goalkeeping legend Bryan Gunn.

How important is it for a goalkeeper to practise kicking and receiving the ball at your feet?

It's more important now than it was 10 years ago especially if your manager wants to play out from the back. More and more teams are now playing that way so you need to practice by kicking and receiving the ball from a young age. This should make you more comfortable having the ball at your feet in a match. Don't forget though, a goalkeeper's main aim is still to keep the ball out of the net.

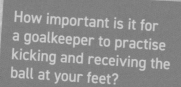

Where should a goalkeeper position themselves when the opponent is shooting?

This depends on where the ball is and where your defenders are. If your defenders are deep you don't want to be standing too high in your six-yard box because your reaction time will become less. Make sure your steps are short and sharp, follow the ball and make sure you're not moving when the player kicks the ball. When you see them take their leg back you need to stop because if you're moving when they strike it you will find it hard to adjust and save it. So stay still and be ready to go either way.

Can you explain the importance of communicating with your teammates..?

You can see the whole match in front of you so it's important to speak with your defenders. Try to give them any information on where they should be and where the opposition players are. Also tell them if they have time or if they need to clear the ball. It's half your work as if you communicate well to your defenders you will have to make less saves.

How do you bounce back from making a mistake?

It's the worst feeling making a mistake as a goalkeeper because it usually ends in a goal. If you make an error you just have to take as many positives from it as possible. If you learn from them you'll be less likely to make the same mistake again which is the main thing. You must also realise that you will make mistakes but see them all as learning curves and something you can view as a positive.

What advice would you give on how to catch a high ball?

The main thing is to try and not move too early. Any little movement the wrong way can put you out of position. Try to be patient and pick up the ball flight as early as you can. When you move you have to move as late and fast as you possibly can. If you move too early the opposition player might outjump you. Keep an eye on the ball, stay strong and get a good jump so you can take the ball as high as possible.

What can a goalkeeper do in a one vs one situation to gain an advantage?

Don't go down too early. A lot of players will try to give you a dummy or take it round you so if you go down early it will make it easier for them to score. Try not to stand too high up or too close to your line because it will make it easier for them to shoot past you. Make sure you're in a good position, on your feet and stand as big as you can. Be ready to save a shot with your arms, legs, feet, or to block it if the player tries to take it round you.

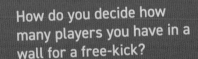

How do you decide how many players you have in a wall for a free-kick?

If the free-kick is being taken between the lines of your six-yard box then you will definitely need at least four players in the wall. Then between the six-yard and the 18-yard box you can go for a three-man wall. Any wider than that you'll just want to have one or two. A lot depends on how far out the free-kick is but goalkeepers tend to stick to these guidelines.

You've saved penalties in your career. How do you try to gain an advantage in that situation?

It's very hard to save penalties but try to watch the opposition players during the game as you could pick up where they like to shoot the ball. During a penalty it's good to throw in a counter movement where you make the taker think you're going to go one way but then go the opposite way. If you can save a penalty it's a bonus because you're not expected to.

Where do you stand when facing a free-kick?

Stand to the opposite side of the goal the wall is protecting. Stay still as the free-kick is being taken and try to make the save if it passes the wall. If it goes in the goal over the wall then it's not the goalkeeper's fault but if it goes around the wall and towards the side you're standing then you will be expected to save it.

ONES TO WATCH

EUROPE'S NEW KIDS ON THE BLOCK

Each year a crop of talented youngsters start to make a real name for themselves. Here are eight talented prospects that have what it takes to become one of the best in the Premier League...

REISS NELSON

POSITION:
Midfielder

DATE OF BIRTH:
December 10, 1999

FACT: Scored seven Bundesliga goals in the 2018/19 season during a loan spell at Hoffenheim from Arsenal.

ERIC GARCIA

POSITION: Centre-back

DATE OF BIRTH: January 9, 2001

FACT: Played both legs of Manchester City's League Cup semi-final win against Burton Albion in 2019.

LLOYD KELLY

POSITION: Left-back

DATE OF BIRTH: October 1, 1998

FACT: Bournemouth paid Bristol City £13million to buy Kelly in May 2019.

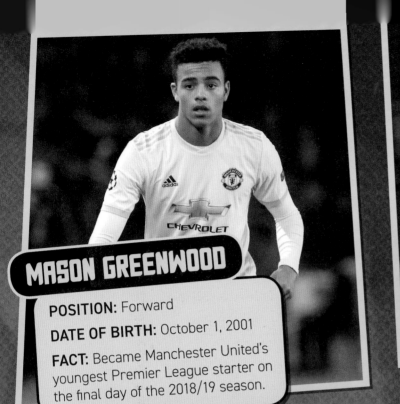

MASON GREENWOOD

POSITION: Forward

DATE OF BIRTH: October 1, 2001

FACT: Became Manchester United's youngest Premier League starter on the final day of the 2018/19 season.

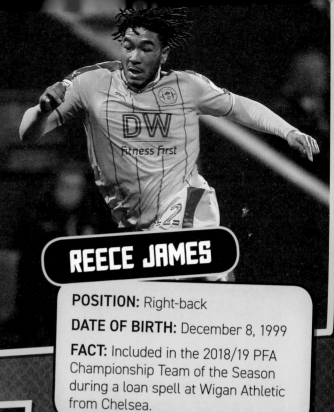

REECE JAMES

POSITION: Right-back

DATE OF BIRTH: December 8, 1999

FACT: Included in the 2018/19 PFA Championship Team of the Season during a loan spell at Wigan Athletic from Chelsea.

RHIAN BREWSTER

POSITION: Striker

DATE OF BIRTH: April 1, 2000

FACT: Won a Champions League winner's medal with Liverpool in 2019.

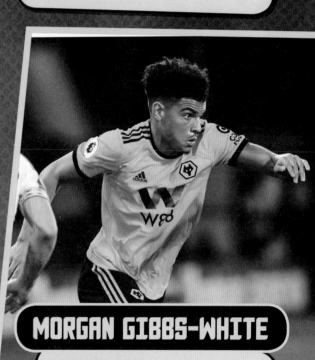

MORGAN GIBBS-WHITE

POSITION: Midfielder

DATE OF BIRTH: January 27, 2000

FACT: Made 26 Premier League appearances for Wolverhampton Wanderers in the 2018/19 season.

MAX AARONS

POSITION: Right-back

DATE OF BIRTH: January 4, 2000

FACT: Helped Norwich City win the Championship in his first season as a professional.

SPOT THE STARS!

Seven of France's 2018 World Cup winning squad have gone for a day out to watch the football. Can you find them enjoying themselves in the crowd?

PAUL POGBA

ANTOINE GRIEZMANN

N'GOLO KANTE

KYLIAN MBAPPE

SAMUEL UMTITI

OLIVIER GIROUD

HUGO LLORIS

ANSWERS ON PAGE 77

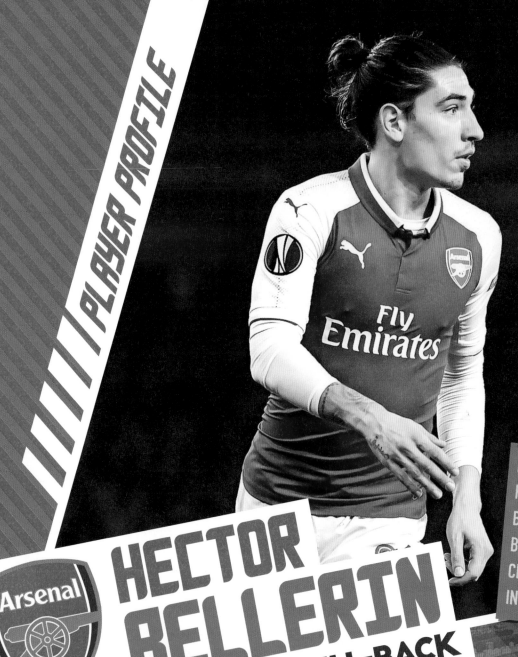

HECTOR BELLERIN

ARSENAL'S FLYING FULL-BACK

FACT FILE

POSITION: Right-back
HEIGHT: 1.78m (5ft 8in)
BIRTH DATE: March 19, 1995
BIRTH PLACE: Barcelona, Spain
CLUB: Arsenal
INTERNATIONAL: Spain

Arsenal's Spanish right-back Hector Bellerin has been getting fans in the Emirates off their seats since making his debut back in 2013.

But what you might not know is that the Gunners star didn't start his football career in North London. Bellerin spent eight years in Barcelona's youth academy before moving to Arsenal in the summer of 2011.

Then boss Arsene Wenger persuaded the highly-rated defender to leave his boyhood club by promising him a fast-track to first-team football.

After impressing in the Gunners' youth teams, it wasn't too long before Wenger delivered on his promise.

In September 2013 – just two months after signing his first professional deal - the then 18-year-old made his senior debut in a League Cup victory at West Bromwich Albion.

After his debut, the highly-rated European teenager's next experience of senior football was to move away from the Emirates in a loan spell with the then Championship side Watford.

In two separate back-to-back spells at Vicarage Road, he made eight appearances for the Hornets. It was a short but valuable learning experience.

When he returned to Arsenal for 2014/15 pre-season, Bellerin famously beat Theo Walcott's 40-metre sprint record by 0.01 seconds which saw him labelled as one of the 'fastest players in the world'.

Despite his lightning speed and talent, Mathieu Debuchy, Calum Chambers and Nacho Monreal were all ahead of Hector for a place at full-back.

However, injuries to all three resulted in Wenger handing the speed king his Champions League debut in a 2-0 defeat to Borussia Dortmund in September.

Despite the loss it was the beginning of something big for the Spaniard as he started to slowly establish himself.

Five months later – and now a regular in the squad - Hector scored his first goal for the club in a 5-0 win over Aston Villa, before picking up his first silverware as Arsenal beat the same opponent 4-0 in the FA Cup final.

Forty-four appearances and a place in the PFA Team of the Year followed the next season but, despite lifting the Community Shield in August, Arsenal failed to win a major trophy.

That failure to win a big trophy was put right when Bellerin's hands were once again on the FA Cup after victory over Chelsea in May 2017.

But following a second Community Shield victory – once again against Chelsea – the Spaniard hasn't got his hands on a team honour since with Arsenal losing the 2017/18 League Cup final 3-0 to Manchester City the closest he's come.

The flying full-back has also not played in the Champions League since the 2016/17 campaign after failing to qualify for three successive years despite going close in Unai Emery's first season at the helm.

When the current boss replaced Arsene Wenger in the summer of 2018, many predicted that his fellow Spaniard Hector would take his performances up another level.

But just 19 matches under the guidance of his new manager, the defender suffered a ruptured anterior cruciate knee ligament which ruled him out for nine months.

It's an injury that has ended careers but Emery believes that the gutsy right-back has returned to his squad "stronger than before."

If one thing is for sure, Arsenal are certainly more of a force and a better team when Hector Bellerin is on the pitch.

INTERNATIONAL

Bellerin had a standout international career for Spain's youth teams but has yet to establish himself at senior level like many predicted.

He reached the 2013 European Championship semi-finals with the Under-19s and was named in the Team of the Tournament.

Three years later he was handed his full international debut by Vicente del Bosque against Bosnia & Herzegovina.

The World Cup and Euro 2012 winning boss then included the Arsenal man in his 23-man squad for Euro 2016 but he failed to make an appearance in France.

Since then he's been overlooked by both coaches Julen Lopetegui and Luis Enrique but there's no doubt that the 24-year-old still has plenty of time to make a real impression on the international stage.

DID YOU KNOW?

Bellerin loves his fashion and is often attending events. He likes to wear the latest styles and will often share these on Instagram.

Instagram: @hectorbellerin
Twitter: @HectorBellerin

TARGET 10

A

B

Look closely at the two sets of images below. You may think they are the same but there are actually 10 differences between picture A to picture B. Can you spot them all?

ANSWERS ON PAGE 77

A

B

39

EURO 2020 GROUND GAME

The European Championship takes place in the summer of 2020. Twelve cities in 12 different countries will host the tournament. Can you link the stadium name to the correct image...?

Krestovsky Stadium (Saint Petersburg, Russia) 68,134

San Mames (Bilbao, Spain) 53,332

Wembley Stadium (London, England) 90,000

A:

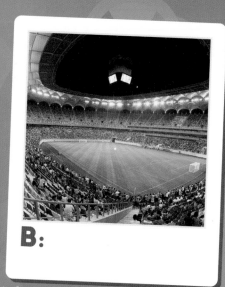

B:

C:

D:

Parken Stadium (Copenhagen, Denmark) 38,065

Hampden Park (Glasgow, Scotland) 52,063

Johan Cruyff Arena (Amsterdam, Netherlands) 54,990

E:

40

F:

G:

H:

I:

K:

L:

J:

ANSWERS ON PAGE 77

41

CHELSEA
FOOTBALL CLUB

FACT FILE

POSITION: Forward
HEIGHT: 1.59m (5ft 3in)
BIRTH DATE: July 19, 1998
BIRTH PLACE: Irvine, Scotland
CLUB: Chelsea
INTERNATIONAL: Scotland

DID YOU KNOW?

Cuthbert has scored in the Champions League, European Championship, World Cup, FA Cup, Women's Super League and WSL Cup.

ERIN CUTHBERT

SCOTLAND'S SUPER STRIKER

There's no doubt that Erin Cuthbert is one of the most exciting talents in the Women's Super League.

Since moving from Glasgow City to Chelsea the determined forward has already established herself as a key player in a squad full of superstars.

Despite narrowly missing out on silverware in 2018/19 after three semi-final defeats, the Irvine-born star was included in the PFA Team of the Year following an impressive personal campaign.

Cuthbert, who is only 21, was also nominated for both the PFA Player and Young Player of the Year Awards and named Chelsea's Player of the Year.

Now the Scotland ace spoke exclusively to Shoot about playing for Chelsea, personal recognition and her pride in representing the Tartan Army.

Did you always dream of becoming a footballer?

"I always grew up with the dream that I could become a professional footballer. Scotland's all-time leading scorer Julie Fleeting lived in my local area and I often saw her around so I knew it was something that could be achieved."

Who were your idols growing up?

"From the men's game it has to be Lionel Messi. He's the greatest of all time. I haven't seen anyone dribble the way he does. From the women's game it's Julie Fleeting. She was the local hero when I was growing up. I walked out with her as a mascot in 2007 and idolised everything about her."

What's it been like since moving from Scotland to Chelsea?

"The time I've been here has gone so quickly and tells me how short of a career football is. I just really enjoy it here and make every moment count. I spend more time with the team than my family. They are not only my teammates but also my best friends."

What's it like to be part of a team that's won WSL titles and the FA Cup?

"Crazy! I'm not surprised because we have so much quality in the team. There's lots of international talent but we've found a way to fit together and a way to win. It doesn't matter who's in the starting XI because it's all about the squad coming together as one."

What's it like to train and play with top players like Ji So-Yun and Fran Kirby?

"Great because it only helps me improve. There's so much attacking talent at Chelsea so I knew what I was getting into when I joined the club. It took a little bit of time to make my mark but in my second season I almost played every game. I've worked tirelessly to continuously improve aspects of my game to keep up with the competition around me."

Chelsea lost three semi-finals in the 2019 season. How tough was that to take?

"Very tough. We put a lot of our energy into the Champions League because we really felt we could win it. We had the chances to beat Lyon and felt we deserved it over both games. It really hurt not to win any trophies after coming so close but we've definitely improved as a team. I think our squad is stronger than when we won the double in 2018 but we didn't quite get the luck."

What was it like to be named in the PFA Team of the Year, plus nominated for the Player and Young Player of the Year Awards?

"I was shocked, surprised and humbled. I didn't know I had made that much of an impression on my fellow professionals. To be nominated and be in the Team of the Year is a great achievement and honour but it doesn't mean anything when the team hasn't won any trophies. I play football because it's a team sport and I want to win trophies."

How would you describe your playing style?

"Fearless. It doesn't matter who I'm coming up against or how prestigious they are because they are just another footballer to me. I just give my best in every single game and hope that if I leave everything out on the pitch that it will be good enough."

How much of an honour is it to play for Scotland?

"For me there's no better feeling in the whole wide world. Everything I do for my club is to prepare me to play for my country. Every time I put on the shirt I feel a sense of responsibility because as a young girl I used to look up to the players as role models. I know I need to perform but also inspire young girls to play football."

What was it like to score Scotland's first ever major tournament goal at Euro 2017?

"It was a great feeling when the ball went in. I came off the bench and I just wanted to change the game because it was 1-0 to Portugal. When it went in I saw so many Scotland fans celebrating and it was great to have my family in the crowd to see that moment."

How exciting was it to play at the 2019 World Cup in France?

"I can't even put into words how exciting it was. As a little kid I dreamed of playing in a World Cup but Scotland Women had never qualified for a major tournament so I'm lucky that we did it in 2017 and in 2019. It's hard to put into words and I hope it kickstarts the generation of young girls in Scotland wanting to become footballers."

How are you still trying to improve your game?

"I think I can score more. I try to do a lot of shooting and recently I've been taking a lot of set pieces so I've been staying after training to work on those. As small as I am I would also like to be better in the air so I can score more goals with my head. Most of the ones I score with my head are lucky!"

What advice can you give any young Shoot reader dreaming of becoming a footballer?

"Believe you can do it. Don't listen to anyone who tells you your dream isn't possible because you can achieve it if you set your mind to it. I had a dream and thanks to the support of my friends and family I'm now managing to live it."

QUICK FIRE

Go-to meal? Chicken stir-fry.

Favourite goal you've scored? For Scotland v Argentina at the World Cup.

What do you do when you're not playing? I'm studying for a business degree. I'm realistic that football is a short career.

Pre-match track? 'Alive' by Chase & Status

One to watch? Lauren James (Manchester United) – she's got the world at her feet.

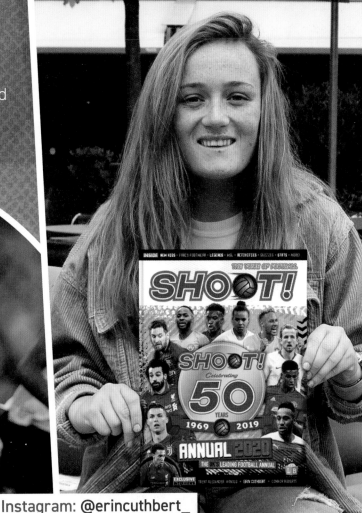

Instagram: @erincuthbert_
Twitter: @erincuthbert_

45

WSL SUPER7

The birth of the Women's Super League in 2011 has really taken women's football in the UK to the next level. Now a majority of the world's best players are playing in this country and top homegrown talent is staying put. But who are the WSL's leading superstars? With so many world-class players that's a difficult question to answer but here are seven standout performers...

STEPH HOUGHTON

CLUB: Manchester City
POSITION: Defender
BIRTH DATE: April 23, 1988
BIRTH PLACE: Durham

Manchester City's versatile leader Steph Houghton is a cut above the rest in the Women's Super League. Her pace, power and leadership qualities mean that the England captain is a rock-solid centre-back and a frightening opponent. But the three-time WSL winner is not just a great defender, she also has an eye for a goal. From direct and indirect set plays, the fan favourite is a constant threat. Her ability at both ends of the pitch should not be underestimated.

JORDAN NOBBS

CLUB: Arsenal
POSITION: Midfielder
BIRTH DATE: December 8, 1992
BIRTH PLACE: Stockton-on-Tees

When former Arsenal Ladies manager Vic Ackers substituted on a 17-year-old midfielder in the Champions League back in 2010, there was always the feeling that this hard-working, gifted player would become something special. A decade on she has fulfilled that potential with three WSL winners' medals and over 50 England caps. This ball-winning, creative spark is the player every club desires to have in the centre of the park.

FRAN KIRBY

CLUB: Chelsea
POSITION: Forward
BIRTH DATE: June 29, 1993
BIRTH PLACE: Reading

Energetic, creative and passionate are three words that you can use to describe every single Fran Kirby performance. The forward is blessed with speed and quick-feet, allowing her to beat her defender and break through the opposition lines. The 2018 FWA and PFA Player of the Year has been a key player for England since making her debut in 2014. After years of incredible success, filled with plenty of important goals and assists, it would not be the magnificent seven without the deadly Reading-born playmaker.

FARA WILLIAMS

CLUB: Reading
POSITION: Midfielder
BIRTH DATE: January 25, 1984
BIRTH PLACE: London

It will come as no surprise to see England's most capped player in history with 168 games make our list. Fara Williams won two WSL titles with Liverpool and has also played for Everton, Arsenal and now Reading in the top-tier. Her flair, set-piece wizardry and superb dribbling has meant that she is able to create from anywhere. A player who can sit deep and pick passes but also with a willingness to create and push into the number 10 role means that the Reading playmaker is always one of the first names on the teamsheet.

KATIE ZELEM

CLUB: Manchester United
POSITION: Midfielder
BIRTH DATE: January 20, 1996
BIRTH PLACE: Oldham

In true Paul Pogba style, Zelem left Manchester United and returned a few seasons later from Juventus as a gifted, quick-thinking midfield maestro. The 23-year-old is superb from dead ball scenarios, whipping in lethal crosses or finding the back of the net. In the Red Devils' first season she was named the club's Player of the Year after her 11 goals saw United win promotion from WSL Championship. As this bright prospect plays regular top-tier football don't be surprised to see her follow the footsteps of her idol Fara Williams in an England shirt.

VIVIANNE MIEDEMA

CLUB: Arsenal
POSITION: Striker
BIRTH DATE: July 15, 1996
BIRTH PLACE: Hoogeveen, Netherlands

Since making her professional debut for Heerenveen at the age of 15, Vivanne Miedema has been setting the world of women's football alight. Arguably the best penalty box finisher in the game, her 81 goals in four years at Bayern Munich and Arsenal helped deliver a WSL, WSL Cup and two Bundesliga titles. By 22 the Dutch sharp-shooter had already lifted the European Championship trophy and become her country's leading scorer after surpassing 59 goals. This powerful centre forward is an immense physical presence, and demonstrates great vision and intelligent movement.

JI SO-YUN

CLUB: Chelsea
POSITION: Midfielder
BIRTH DATE: February 21, 1991
BIRTH PLACE: Seoul, South Korea

A brilliant selfless team player, it is surprising that So-Yun is the all-time leading scorer for South Korea. But that is until you remember that the Chelsea midfielder has the ability to create a chance out of nothing and is blessed with the sweetest of strikes. Since moving to England from Japan in 2014, the Korean superstar has won two WSL and FA Cup doubles. The 2015 PFA Player of the Year is always a constant threat to the opposition, both on and off the ball with her eye for a pass and intelligent movement.

WHICH BALL?

You will see six footballs in each of the following four photos. It's your task to choose which you think is the real one. Write your answers in the space below each action packed image.

ANSWERS ON PAGE 77

GAME 1: LEICESTER CITY V CHELSEA

GAME 2: HUDDERSFIELD TOWN V MANCHESTER UNITED

GAME 3: NEWCASTLE UNITED V LIVERPOOL

GAME 4: TOTTENHAM HOTSPUR V LEICESTER CITY

2019 WINNERS

The past 12 months has been filled with success for a number of teams. Here's a list of the big UK, Europe and international winners. Fill in the blanks once all the competitions have finished.

DOMESTIC

PREMIER LEAGUE, FA CUP, LEAGUE CUP
Manchester City

CHAMPIONSHIP
1st: Norwich City,
Promoted - Sheffield United,
Aston Villa (play-offs)

SCOTTISH PREMIER LEAGUE, SCOTTISH CUP, SCOTTISH LEAGUE CUP
Celtic

LEAGUE ONE
1st: Luton Town,
Promoted - Barnsley,
Charlton Athletic (play-offs)

LEAGUE TWO
1st: Lincoln City,
Promoted - Bury, MK Dons,
Tranmere Rovers (play-offs)

NIFL PREMIERSHIP
Linfield
WELSH PREMIER LEAGUE
The New Saints

NATIONAL LEAGUE
1st: Leyton Orient,
Promoted – Salford City
(play-offs)

STILL TO COME
COMMUNITY SHIELD

EUROPE

LIGUE 1 (France)
Paris Saint-Germain

LA LIGA (Spain)
FC Barcelona

SERIE A (Italy)
Juventus

EREDIVISIE (Netherlands)
Ajax

PRIMEIRA LIGA (Portugal)
Benfica

CHAMPIONS LEAGUE
Liverpool

EUROPA LEAGUE
Chelsea

STILL TO COME
EUROPEAN SUPER CUP

WOMEN

WSL
Arsenal

WSL CUP, FA CUP
Manchester City

WSL CHAMPIONSHIP
1st: Manchester United, Promoted - Tottenham Hotspur

INTERNATIONAL

ASIAN CUP
Qatar

ASIAN GAMES
South Korea

NATIONS LEAGUE
Portugal

STILL TO COME

WOMEN'S WORLD CUP

AFRICA CUP OF NATIONS

CONCACAF GOLD CUP

COPA AMERICA

MAGICAL MESSI
600 NOT OUT!

The year 2019 was yet another outstanding one from the magical Lionel Messi.

Top scorer in both La Liga and the Champions League for the sixth time with 36 goals in Spain and 12 in Europe, the Argentinian ace shows no sign of slowing down despite turning 32 in June.

Remarkably the famous number 10 racked up his 600th goal for FC Barcelona as he fired home a world-class free-kick against Liverpool in the Champions League semi-final.

Messi reached this milestone in his 14th full season as a professional meaning he's averaged over 42 goals a year. Incredible!

Leo also won his 10th La Liga title as the Catalan giants comfortably defended their domestic league crown.

Despite Liverpool's amazing comeback and a Spanish Cup final defeat to Valencia, Messi's 51 goals in all competitions again has many labelling him as football's GOAT (greatest of all time).

Juventus and Portugal superstar Cristiano Ronaldo has certainly been a close rival for that title, while the likes of Diego Maradona, Pele, Johan Cruyff, Michel Platini and Franz Beckenbauer also have a case.

But if you take a look at the following mind-boggling numbers, it's hard to argue that there has been someone better than Messi to play the beautiful game.

THE GOAT?
MESSI IN NUMBERS

GOALS

FC Barcelona	Argentina
2004/05 – 1	2006 – 2
2005/06 – 8	2007 – 6
2006/07 – 17	2008 – 2
2007/08 – 16	2009 – 3
2008/09 – 38	2010 – 2
2009/10 – 48	2011 – 4
2010/11 – 53	2012 – 12
2011/12 – 73	2013 – 6
2012/13 – 60	2014 – 8
2013/14 – 41	2015 – 4
2014/15 – 58	2016 – 8
2015/16 – 41	2017 – 4
2016/17 – 54	2018 – 4
2017/18 – 45	2019 – 3
2018/19 – 51	
TOTAL – 604	TOTAL – 68

FOR FC BARCELONA:

- **687** SECOND MOST GAMES (behind Xavi)
- **603** MOST GOALS
- **371** GOALS AHEAD OF NEXT TOP SCORER (Cesar)
- **175** MOST ASSISTS
- **112** MOST CHAMPIONS LEAGUE GOALS
- **70** MOST PENALTY GOALS
- **45** MOST HAT-TRICKS
- **42** MOST FREE-KICK GOALS
- **26** MOST GOALS IN EL CLASICO (vs Real Madrid)
- **10** LA LIGA TITLES
- **8** MOST HAT-TRICKS IN ONE LA LIGA SEASON
- **7** SPANISH SUPER CUP TITLES
- **6** COPA DEL REY TITLES
- **5** MOST GOALS IN A CHAMPIONS LEAGUE GAME (vs Bayer Leverkusen 2012)
- **4** CHAMPIONS LEAGUE TITLES
- **3** EUROPEAN SUPER CUP & CLUB WORLD CUP TITLES

OTHER NUMBERS:

- **419** MOST LA LIGA GOALS
- **166** MOST LA LIGA ASSISTS
- **91** MOST GOALS IN ONE YEAR (2012)
- **73** MOST GOALS IN ONE SEASON (2011/12)
- **50** MOST GOALS IN ONE LA LIGA SEASON (2011/12)
- **14** MOST CHAMPIONS LEAGUE GOALS IN ONE SEASON (2011/12)
- **12** MOST FIFPRO WORLD XI APPEARANCES (joint with Cristiano Ronaldo)
- **11** MOST ARGENTINA FOOTBALLER OF THE YEAR AWARDS
- **10** SECOND MOST UEFA TEAM OF THE YEAR APPEARANCES (behind Cristiano Ronaldo)
- **8** MOST LA LIGA BEST PLAYER & BEST FORWARD AWARDS
- **6** MOST EUROPEAN GOLDEN SHOE AWARDS, LA LIGA & CHAMPIONS LEAGUE TOP SCORER
- **5** MOST BALLON D'OR AWARDS (joint with Cristiano Ronaldo)
- **3** MOST UEFA GOAL OF THE SEASON AWARDS
- **2** MOST CLUB WORLD CUP GOLDEN BALLS

FOR ARGENTINA:

- **132** THIRD MOST CAPS (behind Javier Mascherano and Javier Zanetti)
- **68** MOST GOALS
- **18** YOUNGEST PLAYER TO PLAY AND SCORE AT THE WORLD CUP (2006)
- **13** MOST PENALTY GOALS
- **12** MOST GOALS IN ONE YEAR (2012 – joint with Gabriel Batistuta)
- **6** MOST FREE-KICK GOALS & HAT-TRICKS
- **1** WORLD CUP GOLDEN BALL AWARDS, 2008 OLYMPIC GOLD MEDAL, 2005 UNDER-20 WORLD CUP

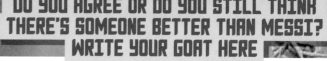

DO YOU AGREE OR DO YOU STILL THINK THERE'S SOMEONE BETTER THAN MESSI? WRITE YOUR GOAT HERE

Stats correct at the end of the 2018/19 season

Connor Roberts has had a whirlwind 18 months. The right-back has played in the Premier League and become a regular at both club and international level. The proud Welshman spoke to Shoot about representing his hometown club, playing for a legend and how he once played with a different shaped ball altogether.

DID YOU KNOW?

Connor also played cricket for local team Llandarcy and was an all-rounder.

EXCLUSIVE

CONNOR ROBERTS

ROBERTS' RAPID RISE

What has the last 18 months been like?

"It's been amazing. I was in a dark place on loan at Middlesbrough, not playing and I had just a year left on my contract with Swansea. I was questioning whether I was good enough. Then Angel Rangel came off injured in the Premier League and I went back to Swansea as quick as I could. Luckily the manager Carlos Carvalhal put me in the team for the next match and since then I've managed to stay in."

How proud are you to represent Wales?

"To play for Wales is unbelievable. Every game could be my last so I just enjoy every single moment I get to play for my country. My dad used to say I was good enough to play for Wales but he meant in rugby so it's funny that I'm representing them in football now. I just like to go out there, enjoy myself and make my family proud."

What's it like to play for Welsh legend Ryan Giggs?

"When you're in a team meeting and realise you're sitting there listening to Ryan Giggs it's mad. When I was younger I used to watch him on TV playing for Man United teams that were winning everything so I didn't think I'd ever be playing for him. I look up to him and I take everything he has to offer. Every time I go away with Wales it's great to be able to learn from and be in the presence of someone who's achieved pretty much everything in his career."

How inspiring are senior teammates like Aaron Ramsey and Gareth Bale?

"It's massive because there's a lot of young players in the squad. If you see what they have achieved for Wales they are definitely a big inspiration to me. They have had really good careers and are really good players. If I could get anywhere near what those guys have achieved then I'd be over the moon."

How exciting is it for Wales at the moment with so much talent in the squad?

"It's huge for Wales. We've got David Brooks, Ethan Ampadu, Daniel James, Harry Wilson and other talented young players in the squad. They're hungry to replicate what the older players did at the Euros a few years ago and what they've achieved in their careers. It's exciting times but we know there's a lot of hard work that needs to be done if we want to get to where we want to be as a national team."

QUICK FIRE

Favourite TV show: Line of Duty

Player you looked up to as a youngster: Angel Rangel. I learnt a lot from him

Pre-match track: 'Clarity' by Zedd.

Favourite video game: Fortnite

Pre-match meal: Salmon and sweet potato or spaghetti and tomato sauce

Can you share how you may have had a career in a different sport...?

"I played rugby for Wales when I was 10 years old. I was probably better at rugby than football when I was younger but I was too small and didn't really grow enough so I decided to give football a go. Luckily it paid off."

Do you set yourself goals for the future?

"I just take each game and opportunity I get as it comes. The only aim I really have is to keep working hard and improving. Hopefully I can then stay involved with Wales on a regular basis and help them qualify for Euro 2020 next summer."

What advice would you give to young Shoot readers dreaming of playing football?

"Never give up. I've had setbacks in my career but I've always believed in my ability. You just have to work hard, enjoy yourself and if it's meant to be then it's meant to be."

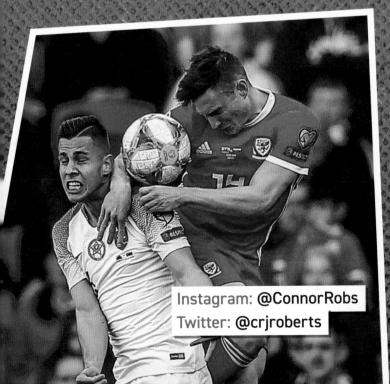

Instagram: @ConnorRobs
Twitter: @crjroberts

SHOOT! TURNS 50

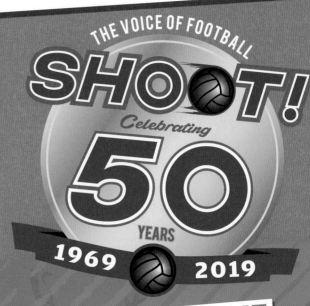

SHOOT!

Celebrating

50 YEARS

1969 — 2019

In case you didn't know, Shoot – The Voice of Football – celebrated its 50th birthday in 2019.

To celebrate our big anniversary, we look back at some historic milestones and iconic covers from over the past half century.

SHOOT ONLINE

Website – shoot.co.uk
Twitter - @_shootfootball
Facebook - @TheVoiceOfFootball

TIMELINE

1969
The first ever Shoot magazine is published by IPC Media on August 13th. The debut edition featured the famous League Ladders, 'You Are The Ref' comic strip and a guest column penned by England's World Cup winning captain Bobby Moore.

1975
Shoot's weekly edition was firmly established as the UK's most popular football magazine. England internationals Kevin Keegan, Jimmy Greaves and Alan Ball were just three stars to have joined the team as guest writers.

1970
You're currently reading the 2020 edition but the first Shoot Annual (1971) was published back in 1970. Bobby Moore was again the main cover star but this time in his West Ham United kit.

1986
During the 80s Shoot had exclusive inside access to the England camp at both the 1982 and 1986 World Cups via captain Bryan Robson's guest column.

1994
Shoot celebrates its 25th birthday with a special silver anniversary edition.

1996
The weekly features and interviews with the best players in the UK, including stars such as Alan Shearer, Ryan Giggs and Paul Gascoigne, saw sales of Shoot magazine peak at 120,000 copies per week.

2010

Shoot became the first printed football title in the UK to release an online magazine and app.

Little Brother Books publish the UK's Leading Football Annual plus a number of special editions. There's also a website which is updated daily with news and features. www.shoot.co.uk

2008

Pedigree Group Ltd became the new brand owners of Shoot.

ICONIC COVERS

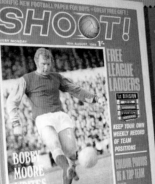

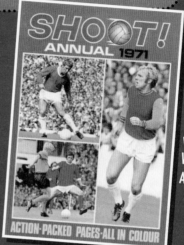

1960s
August 13, 1969 – Shoot magazine launches with Bobby Moore as the cover star.

1970s
The Shoot Annual makes its debut. Bobby Moore (right) again makes the cover along with fellow 1966 World Cup winner Alan Ball (top left).

2001

Like footballer's hairstyles, times change and Shoot magazine moved from a weekly to a monthly edition.

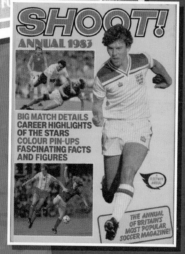

1980s
England star Bryan Robson – nicknamed 'Captain Marvel' – is the main man (right) on the 1983 Annual.

1990s
Then Blackburn Rovers and England striker Alan Shearer (middle) is joined by Manchester United magician Eric Cantona (bottom right) on the 1996 Annual.

1999

Pedigree Group Ltd - the UK's market leader in Annuals – became the publisher of the Shoot Annual. The first cover featured 90s heroes such as David Beckham, Alan Shearer and Dennis Bergkamp.

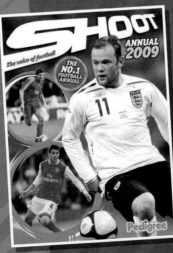

2000s
Wayne Rooney (right), Steven Gerrard (top left) and Cesc Fabregas (bottom left) selected for the cover of the 2009 Annual.

2010s
A different style but the same action-packed features. Marcus Rashford (centre), Jamie Vardy (left), Harry Kane (middle left), Peter Cech (middle right) and Adam Lallana (right) make the 2013 Annual cover squad.

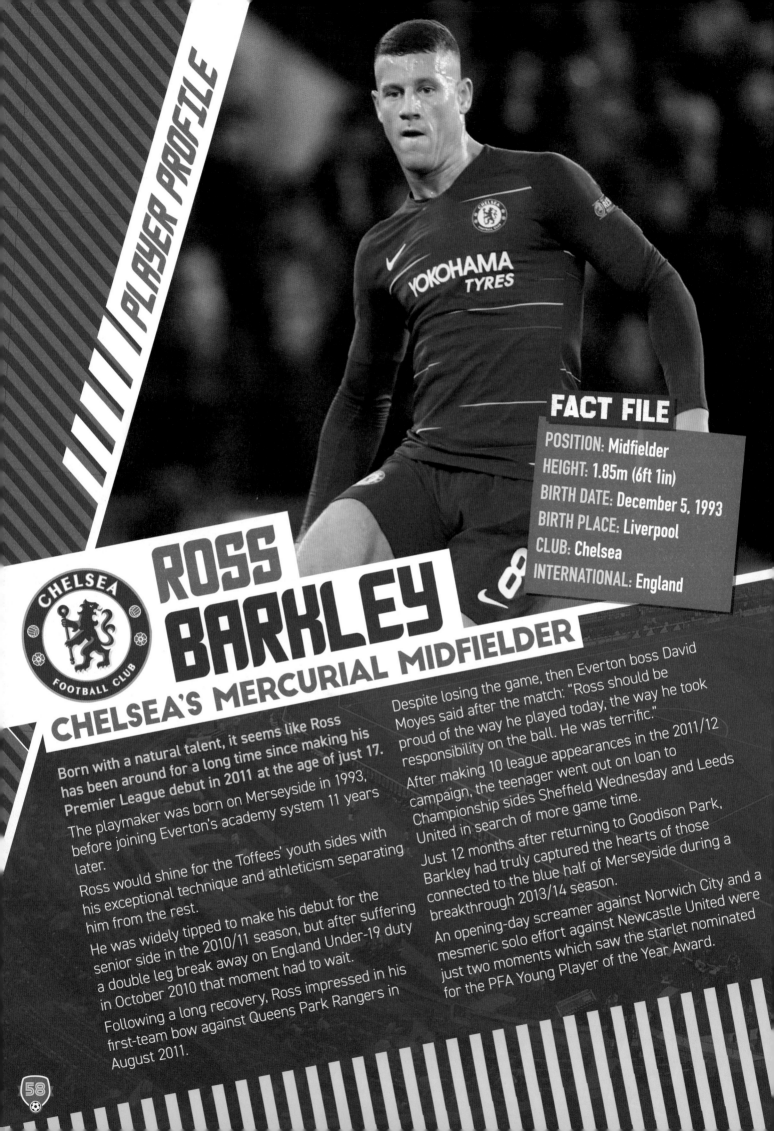

ROSS BARKLEY

CHELSEA'S MERCURIAL MIDFIELDER

FACT FILE

POSITION: Midfielder
HEIGHT: 1.85m (6ft 1in)
BIRTH DATE: December 5, 1993
BIRTH PLACE: Liverpool
CLUB: Chelsea
INTERNATIONAL: England

Born with a natural talent, it seems like Ross has been around for a long time since making his Premier League debut in 2011 at the age of just 17.

The playmaker was born on Merseyside in 1993, before joining Everton's academy system 11 years later.

Ross would shine for the Toffees' youth sides with his exceptional technique and athleticism separating him from the rest.

He was widely tipped to make his debut for the senior side in the 2010/11 season, but after suffering a double leg break away on England Under-19 duty in October 2010 that moment had to wait.

Following a long recovery, Ross impressed in his first-team bow against Queens Park Rangers in August 2011.

Despite losing the game, then Everton boss David Moyes said after the match: "Ross should be proud of the way he played today, the way he took responsibility on the ball. He was terrific."

After making 10 league appearances in the 2011/12 campaign, the teenager went out on loan to Championship sides Sheffield Wednesday and Leeds United in search of more game time.

Just 12 months after returning to Goodison Park, Barkley had truly captured the hearts of those connected to the blue half of Merseyside during a breakthrough 2013/14 season.

An opening-day screamer against Norwich City and a mesmeric solo effort against Newcastle United were just two moments which saw the starlet nominated for the PFA Young Player of the Year Award.

predicted he would become a senior regular by the age of 21.

Ross further raised his profile as the Three Lions won the Under-16 Montaigu Tournament in 2009 and the Under-17 European Championship in 2010.

And after caps at Under-19, Under-20 and Under-21 level, Ross was handed his senior debut at the age of 20 in September 2013 when he came on as a substitute in a 4-0 World Cup qualifier win against Moldova.

An outstanding 2013/14 season was rewarded with a call-up to Roy Hodgson's squad for the 2014 World Cup where he made two appearances before England were knocked out at the group stage.

Now after suffering with injuries and a loss of form, the midfielder has put himself firmly back in the international picture.

With impressive performances, notably against Spain and Montenegro over the past year, Barkley is becoming the player fans hoped he could be.

If he can just keep up his form and get more starts for Chelsea, he could well be a key player for Gareth Southgate at Euro 2020.

Ross was now a regular and the next three seasons saw the attacking midfielder score 15 goals in 103 league appearances for his boyhood club.

But after Roberto Martinez – the man who nurtured Ross into a first-team regular - left the club in 2016, he struggled to regain his previous form.

The local boy's time with the Toffees appeared to be finished after Ronald Koeman's appointment with the Dutch boss trying to play the Englishman on the right-wing.

A move to Chelsea looked set to be completed but when that collapsed he had to return to Everton and wait another four months until the deal went through on January 5, 2018.

So far Ross has had an up and down time in the capital. Although he's shown moments of brilliance, he has not done so enough to earn a regular place in the starting team.

But now in his mid-20s, this is the time for Ross Barkley to show the world why he's previously been compared to Wayne Rooney, Michael Ballack and Paul Gascoigne.

INTERNATIONAL

It was clear for all to see that the Evertonian was a special talent within England's youth ranks and it was

DID YOU KNOW?

Barkley was eligible to represent Nigeria through his grandfather before choosing England.

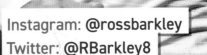

Instagram: @rossbarkley
Twitter: @RBarkley8

SOCIAL SUPERSTARS

We can't get enough of our favourite footballers on social media. Here we take a look at the stars who just love to let their fans know what they are up to away from the pitch.

Manchester United and Liverpool connections getting on. Surely not..?
Credit: @paulpogba

Not a bad motor, Cristiano.
Credit: @cristiano

Can we have a slice please, Luka.
Credit: @lukamodric

That better be a healthy drink, Mesut.
Credit: @m10_official

Imagine if these two had played together.

Credit: @neymarjr

One superhuman is a huge fan of another.

Credit: @leomessi

Dele, give us a song!
Dele, Dele give us a song!

Credit: @dele

When Sancho met Drake.

Credit: @sanchooo10

TOP 5 MOST POPULAR PLAYERS ON INSTAGRAM

CRISTIANO RONALDO
Username:
@cristiano
Followers:
162 million

LIONEL MESSI
Username:
@leomessi
Followers:
122 million

NEYMAR JR
Username:
@neymarjr
Followers:
113 million

DAVID BECKHAM
Username:
@davidbeckham
Followers:
55 million

RONALDINHO
Username:
@ronaldinho
Followers:
44 million

CHELCEE
GRIMES

YOU'LL NEVER WALK ALONE

LIVERPOOL
FOOTBALL CLUB

EST·1892

Multi-talented Scouser Chelcee Grimes has the world at her feet. In the studio, the singer-songwriter is working on her debut album and has written tracks for global superstars such as The Saturdays, Kesha, Dua Lipa and Kylie Minogue.

But when she's not penning songs Chelcee has also played for her beloved Reds, Everton, Tranmere Rovers, Tottenham Hotspur and now Fulham.

The 27-year-old has also performed at the PFA Awards, Liverpool's Champions League final fan zone, and was part of the BBC Sport team at the Women's World Cup in France.

Shoot spoke exclusively to Chelcee about her love for Liverpool, meeting Jurgen Klopp, and the amazing experiences she's had over the past year.

What is your earliest footballing memory?

"The Olympiacos Champions League match at Anfield in 2004. I remember we needed to win by two goals and Steven Gerrard scored a late winner so we won 3-1. I was right behind that goal when it went in."

Why did you choose music over football?

"If I were a boy I probably would've been a footballer now but unfortunately you see everyone else around you getting paid for what they were doing but women footballers weren't back then. Some of the girls went to America but I found music and got my first record deal at 18."

You still play football for Fulham. How do you get the balance right?

"I had to drop down to Fulham because I can only realistically commit to two days a week. But when I do play I love it and the club are really supportive."

Do you go to many matches now?

"Yeah, I still go to matches when I can. I even got to take my younger sister to Anfield last season and we saw Mohamed Salah's screamer against Chelsea. She loved it and is starting to play for her school now."

You've met Jurgen Klopp. Did you get one of his famous hugs?

"I was at Anfield shooting an advert with Jurgen and I did get a little hug at the end. The moment he found out I was a musician he only wanted to speak about music. He told me he's a big fan of Dua Lipa and I told him I've written songs for her. He was amazing and such a laugh. He's brought back what we're about – character. I think we were really missing that before. Scousers have the biggest heart and would do anything for you so when we watch Klopp we really connect with him as a person. I'd love to play for him."

What makes Liverpool FC so magical?

"The history of the club. We haven't won the Premier League since I've been alive but I still love saying 'I support Liverpool'. We have that never say die attitude which we showed in Istanbul in 2005. That sums up the club and the city. It's about believing and dreaming big."

Who are your Liverpool heroes?

"Stevie G is the main one. I met him after we won the Champions League final which was great. At the moment it has to be Mo Salah. I love his story of not making it in the Premier League at first but then he went away, worked hard and came back stronger. I think that reflects me as my first record deal didn't work out but I went away, worked hard and I'm now back in the Premier League."

What did you do after the match?

"I met all of the players and my hero Steven Gerrard after the game. I got a hug from Jurgen, spoke with Andrew Robertson and even got to hold the trophy. I also sang the Mo Salah song with his daughter on stage which was unreal! I'm still on such a high and so proud to be a L iverpool fan."

How great was it to be in Madrid when Liverpool won the Champions League?

"Out of this world! Liverpool fans painted the city red. I actually played to 60,000 fans before the match at the fan park. The police turned the system off after the first song because it was so crazy! So without a microphone I just sang Liverpool songs to the fans. It was unreal. We didn't play that well but I don't care because we won. We deserved to win something and I'm confident we can win the league now."

Which Liverpool player would you choose to do a track with?

"I'd have a little boy band with Alisson on guitar as I know he's quite good at it. I'd also have Alex Oxlade-Chamberlain as he's dating Perrie from Little Mix. Then I'd have Mo Salah doing a rap in the middle just because it's Mo Salah. Sadio Mane could bring some fire at the end."

How exciting is the rise of women's football?

"To see how far it's come is amazing. Watching players that I played with like Nikita Parris, Fara Williams and Alex Greenwood doing so well is exciting. I don't want to put a limit on how far women's football can go but it's growing at a nice pace now. The World Cup showed just that."

Who are your favourite players to watch in the women's game?

"I'd have to say Nikita Parris. She's one of my best friends and is smashing it at club level and for England. To see what she's doing is so exciting and I'm so proud of her. Toni Duggan is another. She's playing for Barcelona and for any player from Liverpool to do that is what dreams are made of."

QUICK FIRE

Favourite stadium (not Anfield)?
Wanda Metropolitano

Best goal you've ever scored?
Overhead kick vs QPR

Favourite pundit? Alex Scott

Pre-match meal? Coffee and yoghurt

Number 1 album or FA Cup winning goal?
Number 1 album

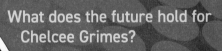

What does the future hold for Chelcee Grimes?

"If you'd told me a few years ago the things that I've now done then I would've laughed. In the future I'd like to be out on tour and keep playing football for as long as I can."

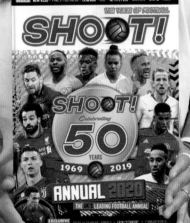

SUPER STRIKERS

Who are the best strikers not playing in the English Premier League? There are so many top forwards around that not everyone will pick the same. We've had a go at choosing six global goal-getters. Do you agree with our selection..?

LIONEL MESSI

Birth Date: June 24, 1987
Birth Place: Rosario, Argentina

Ever since he made his debut in 2004, Lionel Messi has scored over 600 goals for FC Barcelona and has torn defences apart with his almost inhuman skill. The forward has won an armful of honours with FC Barcelona, including 10 La Liga titles and four Champions League trophies. He has also broken countless individual records in the game and has won the Ballon d'Or five times. One of the favourites to win it for a sixth time in 2020, the global icon is arguably the GOAT. Despite his genius on the pitch Argentina's all-time leading scorer hasn't been able to help his country win the World Cup in four attempts. He came closest in 2014 when his team lost 1-0 against Germany in the final.

CRISTIANO RONALDO

Birth Date: February 5, 1985
Birth Place: Funchal, Portugal

The only other player to match Messi's prolific record of five Ballon d'Or wins is Cristiano Ronaldo. The Portugal captain has won league titles in England (Manchester United), Spain (Real Madrid) and Italy (Juventus). He's also won the Champions League five times and is the competition's all-time top goalscorer. Although he was one of the world's best at Old Trafford, Cristiano started to see himself labelled as the GOAT during a remarkable spell at Real Madrid. In his 10 years in Spain he broke every record going and is the club's all-time leading scorer with 450 goals. The Portuguese superstar also helped his country win Euro 2016 and is still producing match-winning performances week after week.

NEYMAR JR.

Birth Date: February 5, 1992
Birth Place: Mogi das Cruzes, Brazil

Brazil's top player is one of the most exciting to watch in world football. After establishing himself as his country's best player with Santos he made the move to Europe with FC Barcelona in 2013. The South American superstar would win two La Liga titles and the Champions League with the Catalan giants before his world-record £200million transfer to Paris Saint-Germain in 2017. He's helped the club win two Ligue 1 crowns meaning he's won titles in his homeland, Spain and France. A maverick of a footballer, Neymar has won the Confederations Cup and 2016 Olympic Games with Brazil in Rio. He's also already scored over 60 goals for his country and will beat Pele's long-standing record of 77 in the coming years.

KYLIAN MBAPPE

Birth Date: December 20, 1998
Birth Place: Paris, France

Despite his age, Kylian Mbappe has already made a case for being one of the best players in the world right now. Starting his career at AS Monaco, his electric pace and deadly finishing helped the club win the Ligue 1 title ahead of Paris Saint-Germain. PSG responded by paying around £155million to take their rival's superstar and he has gone from strength to strength. Two Ligue 1 titles and 57 goals in his first two seasons came either side of an impressive 2018 World Cup. Just 19 at the time, Mbappe scored four goals and was named Best Young Player as Les Bleus won the tournament in Russia. It's amazing what the forward has achieved already and it's exciting to think what he will do over the coming years for his club and country.

ANTOINE GRIEZMANN

Birth Date: March 21, 1991,
Birth Place: Macon, France

A consistent performer for a number of years now, there's no doubt Antoine Griezmann is one of the greatest forwards out there. After five seasons in Real Sociedad's first-team, Atletico Madrid came calling and it was in the capital where he's developed into a one of the world's leading players. The Frenchman has been a key figure in Diego Simeone's side. As well as winning the Europa League and reaching two Champions League finals, the clever attacker has moved into the top-five on the club's all-time leading scorers list. For his country he teamed up perfectly with Mbappe to also score four goals and help France win the 2018 World Cup. Griezmann was also the leading scorer and Player of the Tournament as France finished Euro 2016 runners-up.

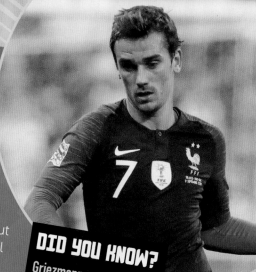

DID YOU KNOW?

Griezmann moved to Spain as a 14-year-old to play for Real Sociedad. He was spotted by the La Liga club playing in a youth tournament in France.

DID YOU KNOW?

Mbappe is only the second teenager to score in a World Cup final. The first was Pele for Brazil in 1958.

DID YOU KNOW?

Robert Lewandowski almost signed for Blackburn Rovers in 2010. He had already held talks with the club but a volcanic ash cloud stopped him from flying.

DID YOU KNOW?

West Ham United bid £12million for Neymar in 2010. His club Santos rejected the offer straight away.

ROBERT LEWANDOWSKI

Birth Date: August 21, 1988
Birth Place: Warszawa, Poland

Poland's prolific superstar Robert Lewandowski has been one of the world's most clinical strikers for a number of years. After scoring 78 times in spells with Znicz Pruszkow and Lech Poznan in his homeland he joined German side Borussia Dortmund in 2010. In four years with Dortmund he fired the club to two Bundesliga titles and a Champions League final. When his contract expired he left for Der Klassiker rivals Bayern Munich in 2014 and has now scored over 200 goals in Germany's top league and has continued to win numerous honours. Lewandowski remarkably struck a record five goals in nine minutes after coming on as a substitute when Bayern beat Wolfsburg 5-1 in 2016. Now Poland's national team captain, he is his country's all-time leading scorer and has played at three major tournaments.

SHOOT'S SUPER

2ND HALF

1

Wolverhampton Wanderers play their home games at which stadium?

2

What is the nickname of Sheffield United?

3

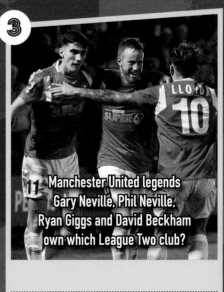

Manchester United legends Gary Neville, Phil Neville, Ryan Giggs and David Beckham own which League Two club?

4

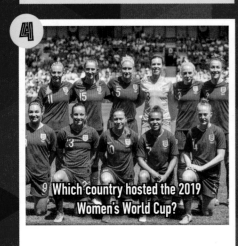

Which country hosted the 2019 Women's World Cup?

5

Aston Villa and which other club played in the 2019 Championship play-off final?

6

At which Premier League team is Alan Shearer a club legend?

7

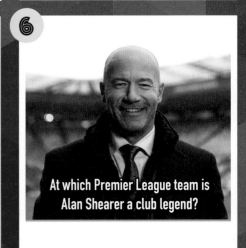

Which number did Aaron Ramsey wear in his last season at Arsenal?

8

Manchester United scored 88, 98 or 108 goals in their Women's Championship winning season?

9

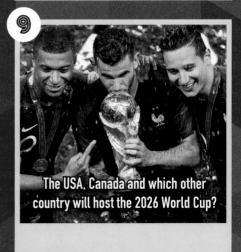

The USA, Canada and which other country will host the 2026 World Cup?

QUIZ

Half time is over. Are you ready for the second half of our ultimate quiz? Remember, you get one point for each correct answer and some can be found in the rest of the annual.

ANSWERS ON PAGE 77

10

What is the nickname of Everton FC?

11

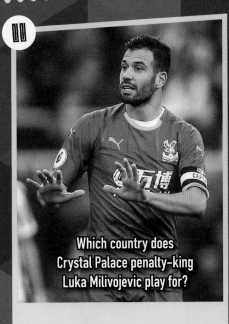

Which country does Crystal Palace penalty-king Luka Milivojevic play for?

12

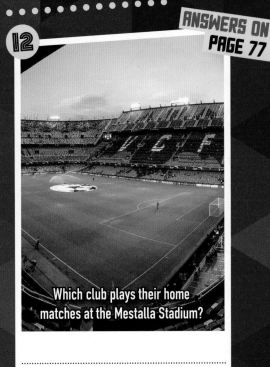

Which club plays their home matches at the Mestalla Stadium?

13

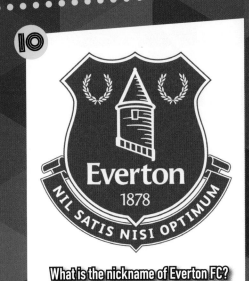

England Women's striker Ellen White moved from Birmingham City to which other club in 2019?

14

TV pundit Jermaine Jenas played 155 Premier League matches for which club?

15

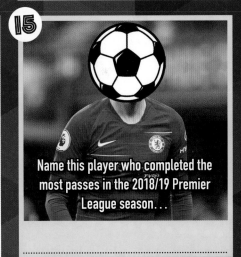

Name this player who completed the most passes in the 2018/19 Premier League season...

16

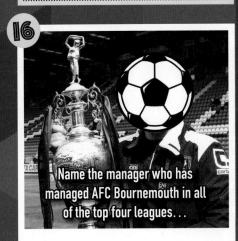

Name the manager who has managed AFC Bournemouth in all of the top four leagues...

17

Lionel Messi scored 41, 51 or 61 goals for FC Barcelona in the 2018/19 season?

18

Arsenal Women's goal-getting forward Vivianne Miedema is from which country?

RAK-SU

WATFORD

It's been a dream few years for Hertfordshire R&B group Rak-Su.

Since winning the 14th series of X-Factor in 2017, Ashley Fongho, Jamaal Shurland, Myles Stephenson and Mustafa Rahimtulla have been as high as number 2 in the UK Singles Chart, toured with Little Mix and Olly Murs, and are close to revealing their debut album.

The boys have also experienced recent success away from music with their local side Watford FC having reached their first FA Cup Final since 1984.

Javi Gracia also guided the Hornets to an 11th placed finish in the Premier League to secure top-flight football at Vicarage Road for a fifth successive season.

Shoot spoke exclusively to the band about their earliest memories of the Hornets, reaching the FA Cup final and which Watford player they'd welcome as the fifth member of Rak-Su.

What's your earliest memories of following Watford?

Myles: "The first ever game I went to was for a school trip and the school was literally a 30-second walk from the stadium. I remember being late and crying because I'd missed a lot. Not the best, but it was my first experience of watching Watford Football Club."

Ashley: "I actually played Sunday league football in Watford and with them being the local team I would go down there to watch games. I don't remember the first match I went to but I've always followed Watford as they are the first team I watched live."

Mustafa: "I think we played Plymouth Argyle in my first Watford game and we drew 1-1. All I remember was thinking this is the team I have to support because I'd just moved to the area. It's good to go and support my local team."

●●●●●●●●●●●●●●●●●●●●●●●●●●●●●●●●

What's your family connection with Watford, Myles...?

"My little brother got signed for Watford when he was seven and, now 17, he's got his scholarship. So as well as following Watford I'm also following my brother's dream."

Who were your Watford icons past and present?

"Marlon King was an absolute baller and Tommy Smith. We also liked Lloyd Doyley. He's a legend at Vicarage Road. Currently I'd say Troy Deeney. He's a real leader for us. Adrian Mariappa is great too. He goes to the same gym as us and the way he carries himself on and off the pitch is so professional."

●●●●●●●●●●●●●●●●●●●●●●●●●●●●●●●●

Any memorable matches or goals that stay with you?

"Deeneyyyy!!! He missed that penalty and then five seconds later Troy's hammered it into the back of the net (vs Leicester City in 2013) to take us to the Championship play-off final. I'd have to say it's one of the best goals of all time."

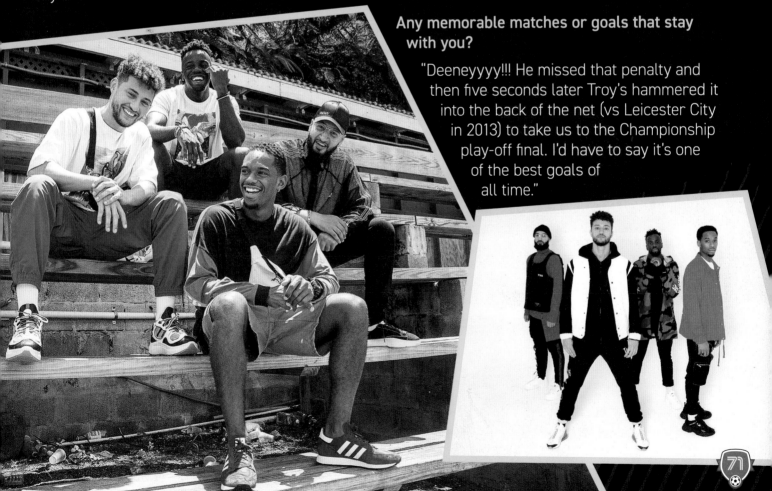

How much are you enjoying the job Javi Gracia is doing at the Vic?

"He's doing an unbelievable job. I think it would have been nice to get the top-10 last season but we just missed out to West Ham on the last day. He got us to the FA Cup final though and we were more than safe in the Premier League which is an unbelievable season for Watford. It will interesting to see where we finish in 2019/20 now."

Despite the defeat to Man City how great was it for the club to reach an FA Cup final?

"It was amazing the fact we reached the final. We would've loved to have been at Wembley for the match but we had a gig at the O2 that night so we couldn't make it. All the Watford fans were having a party, everyone was happy to be there. The score aside, it was a fun day out, everyone had a lot of fun. Man City and Raheem Sterling, who scored twice, were great and they deserved everything they got last season."

We heard Myles and Ashley can play a bit...

Myles: "I aspired to be a footballer growing up. I had a few trials at clubs and played as high as the National League South with Hayes & Yeading. I also had a trial for a team in Greece years ago and a run-out with England schoolboys."

Ashley: "The highest I played was for Chesham United in the Southern Premier Division. We actually got to the FA Cup proper second round one year but I didn't get on the pitch which was kind of upsetting. I also had a few trials when I was younger and played for Watford development for a good few years."

What are your playing styles?

Ashley: "I was never the most gifted person technically so I kind of would play at centre-back or right-back and had the basic understanding of the game. I would be able to read the game and I was a decent athlete but I wasn't the most brilliant on the ball."

Myles: "Growing up I was more of an athlete but, as I've got older, I've become more technical because I don't like running as much. I just tend to stand somewhere and play a ball with my left foot when I get it. So I'd say I'm a flair player now because I just like a nutmeg or to play the perfect defence splitting pass."

Do you both still get time to play?

Myles: "Not that much but Ashley's been playing in his team's cup run. He didn't get to play in the cup final but that's another story. To be fair to him though, he's been playing quite consistently."

Ashley: "I will always play some form of non-league football for as long as I can, whenever I can. Even if it's just with my pals in Watford, if somebody asks me to play football I will always play if I can."

If you had a five-a-side team which current Watford star would be your fifth player?

"Ben Foster. That might be a bit boring but it's pragmatic. With him in a five-a-side goal we would never get beat. We'd win every game 1-0."

● ●

And which Watford player would make a good fifth member of Rak-Su?

"Isaac Success dances in the changing room quite a lot. He has moves and is also built like a brick. Etienne Capoue and Adrian Mariappa seem to have a really good taste in music so I think we'd have to go for one of those three guys."

● ●

What's it like to be alongside Elton John as Watford supporting musicians?

"It's amazing. We've been told that he likes our music and that we're on one of his playlists. Obviously we're nowhere near his level but that's what we're aiming for and hopefully one day we will get there. It puts Watford on the map when someone from Watford comes out and does well. We like to make our friends, family and the local people proud. It's great to bring the community together and give them something to be happy about."

QUICK FIRE

Ultimate GOAT:
Ronaldo (Ashley and Jamaal), Messi (Myles), Mo Salah (Mustafa)

Best at FIFA? Myles

Football stadium you'd love to play a show at? Vicarage Road

Watford 2019/20 finish? 8th

Who out of the four of you would you choose to take an FA Cup winning penalty? Ashley. He put one in top bins at Old Trafford in the 2018 Soccer Aid match.

CHAMPIONS LEAGUE
CAPTION THIS

Football is a funny old game at times. The Shoot team have forgotten to add the captions to these seven hilarious images from the Champions League. Can you help them by filling in the blanks with clever captions? There are no right or wrong answers.

ANSWERS

16-17 SOUTHGATE'S SECRET SELECTION

GK: Pickford
DF: Walker
DF: Gomez
DF: Maguire
DF: Chilwell
MF: Henderson
MF: Winks
MF: Dele
FW: Rashford
FW: Sterling
FW: Kane

08 KNOW YOUR NATIONS

Son Heung-Min — **South Korea**

Pierre-Emerick Aubameyang — **Gabon**

Paulo Dybala — **Argentina**

Christian Pulisic — **USA**

Mat Ryan - **Australia**

Isco - **Spain**

Marquinhos — **Brazil**

09 WORLD CUP WORDSEARCH

D	D	C	J	I	S	L	S	J	R	A	E	Y	Q	O	W	F	B	T	E
Y	B	K	R	G	I	T	W	Z	B	Y	R	Q	K	Q	U	P	L	H	B
K	G	J	J	Z	E	Z	L	H	M	K	C	G	U	U	D	E	B	T	
K	F	Q	A	R	O	A	D	Q	K	G	M	P	E	N	K	C	R	I	L
N	V	R	L	P	T	Q	L	W	W	W	T	O	D	N	I	D	Y	E	Z
Q	D	I	E	X	K	Y	J	F	B	I	M	P	G	E	T	M	Z	J	L
J	N	E	E	K	L	E	I	T	A	L	Y	W	S	K	I	I	R	O	N
G	O	U	D	Y	W	I	T	D	V	G	U	L	Q	S	U	J	U	J	I
D	L	S	X	G	K	S	V	M	Q	V	U	A	E	F	W	J	K	A	F
A	I	A	N	Q	F	F	P	T	P	W	N	O	R	W	A	Y	R	Y	C
S	M	O	O	G	X	Q	T	A	D	N	G	W	S	J	W	Y	L	O	K
K	D	F	R	A	N	C	E	E	I	A	E	D	A	S	Z	Y	R	S	C
I	T	D	D	F	K	J	C	I	O	R	W	S	Y	I	T	N	S	I	
K	A	T	Y	Q	X	M	B	K	S	Q	M	Y	Q	L	N	E	J	M	Y
I	S	S	E	M	A	Z	J	A	R	J	A	W	D	R	T	E	D	U	A
M	N	T	Z	T	N	R	U	Z	S	A	N	O	M	R	D	B	I	U	U
C	S	Q	D	N	Y	K	L	A	D	P	Y	U	E	Y	A	E	C	X	G
L	F	X	J	A	Q	G	O	K	U	A	T	M	U	W	U	E	P	M	U
W	N	E	N	G	L	A	N	D	Y	N	E	D	L	E	C	I	Z	N	
Q	P	U	O	N	J	K	V	X	N	S	Y	B	B	S	N	C	Z	Y	

14 KIT SWAP

Scott Brown — **Shirt C, Shorts A, Socks D**

Jamie Vardy — **Shirt D, Shorts B, Socks A**

Serge Gnabry — **Shirt B, Shorts D, Socks C**

Jordi Alba — **Shirt A, Shorts C, Socks B**

23 WHO AM I?

Ben Foster

Aaron Ramsey

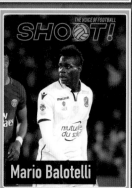
Mario Balotelli

28-29 QUIZ - 1ST HALF

1. Manchester United (13)
2. Republic of Ireland
3. Nikita Parris
4. Fulham
5. Virgil van Dijk
6. Northern Ireland
7. Arsenal
8. Germany
9. Zinedine Zidane
10. Lucy Bronze
11. Sunderland
12. 34
13. Denmark
14. Lyon
15. Gabriel Jesus
16. Shane Long
17. Elland Road
18. Pierre-Emerick Aubameyang

34-35
SPOT THE STARS

38-39 SPOT THE DIFFERENCE

40-41 EURO 2020
GROUND GAME

A. Parken Stadium

B. Arena Nationala

C. Allianz Arena

D. Aviva Stadium

E. San Mames

F. Stadio Olimpico

G. Wembley Stadium

H. Puskas Arena

I. Krestovsky Stadium

J. Hampden Park

K. Olympic Stadium

L. Johan Cruyff Arena

48-49 SPOT THE BALL

GAME 1 – Ball B GAME 3 – Ball C

GAME 2 – Ball D GAME 4 – Ball D

68-69 QUIZ – 2ND HALF

1. Molineux

2. The Blades

3. Salford City

4. France

5. Derby County

6. Newcastle United

7. 8

8. 98

9. Mexico

10. The Toffees

11. Serbia

12. Valencia

13. Manchester City

14. Tottenham Hotspur

15. Jorginho

16. Eddie Howe

17. 51

18. Netherlands

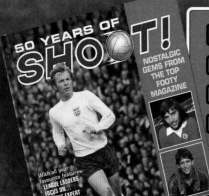